RECYCLING

Learning the Four R's

Reduce, Reuse, Recycle, Recover

Martin J. Gutnik

ENSLOW PUBLISHERS, INC.

Bloy St. & Ramsey Ave.   P.O. Box 38
Box 777   Aldershot
Hillside, NJ 07205   Hants GU12 6BP
U.S.A.   U.K.

Library of Congress Cataloging-in Publication Data

Gutnik, Martin J.
    Recycling: learning the four r's (reduce, reuse, recycle,
recover) / Martin J. Gutnik.
            p. cm.
    Includes bibliographical references and index.
    Summary: Describes different types of trash and where they come from,
their detrimental impact on the environment, and ways recycling can help
solve this problem.
    ISBN 0-89490-399-3
    1. Recycling (waste, etc.)—United States—Juvenile literature.
2. Recycling (Waste, etc.)—United States—Citizen Participation—
Juvenile Literature. [1. Refuse and refuse disposal.
2. Recycling (Waste) 3. Environmental protection.] I. Title
363.72'82—dc20   92-24330
                                                            CIP
                                                            AC

Illustration credits: David Dennis, Tom Stack & Associates, p. 41; Martin J. Gutnik, pp. 13, 18, 24, 26, 28, 47, 50, 73; Bob McKeever, Tom Stack & Associates, p. 65; Gary Milburn, Tom Stack & Associates, p. 33; Milwaukee Department of Recycling, Milwaukee, WI, p. 55; Jack Swenson, Tom Stack & Associates, p. 60; Tom Stack & Associates, p. 39.

Cover Photo: © Greg Vaughn, Tom Stack & Associates

Dedication

To my grandchildren

Joseph Paul Luther and Justin Michael Wiemer

I hope they grow up

in a world that is pure, clean, and free.

Acknowledgment

To my wife, Natalie Browne-Gutnik,

for the many hours of primary research done for this

and many other books

Contents

Introduction

Audubon Woods

In the suburbs of Milwaukee County, Wisconsin, on the shores of Lake Michigan, a small woodlot, approximately forty-two acres of land, is a beautiful example of the interrelationships of nature. Audubon Woods is a section of a deciduous forest—the majority of its trees and shrubs lose their leaves for the winter months. The forest, called a biome, is a community of living organisms and is dependent on a balanced mixture of air, water, soil, and light energy.

For Audubon Woods, this mix of air, water, soil, and light, combined with approximately thirty-five to forty-five inches of rainfall each year, sets the stage for the development of a lush woodland. The woods themselves consist of a wide variety of trees, shrubs, and herbs. These plants grow in a rich, humus soil, with many ponds and many creeks running through it.

In a deciduous forest, there are four layers of plant life. The ground layer consists of herbs and small plants, such as trillium, violets, ferns, and wild onions. Above the ground layer is the shrub layer, with a variety of bushes that grow profusely at the edges of the forest. Honeysuckle, dogwood, raspberry, and blueberry flourish in the shrub layer.

Above stands the understory, consisting of young trees of many varieties. The canopy, the upper layer of the forest, consists of the deciduous trees, which are the dominant life form in the biome. In the Audubon Woods forest, ash, hickory, oak, maple, beech, birch, and elm form the green canopy.

The plants and trees of Audubon Woods provide the habitat for a wide variety of other species. All the species in this forest live in specific areas of the forest called ecosystems. An ecosystem is a specialized part of a biome that contains plant and animal species that live best within that specific area.

One of the ecosystems within Audubon Woods is the boardwalk pond. Here specialized plants, such as algae and elodea, live under the water. Cattails, arrowheads, and rushes grow at the shore. A wide variety of fish and other small aquatic creatures live in the pond and are interrelated through the grazing food chain.

The plants in the pond provide food for all the other living things. Green plants are the only living things on earth that can make food. They do this by using light energy, water, and carbon dioxide to make a simple sugar called glucose.

Many animals in the pond and on its banks eat the green plants. These animals are called herbivores because they only eat green plants. Within the pond, small creatures, called zooplankton, eat the microscopic plants called phytoplankton. Turtles eat the elodea and other submerged plants. Geese and ducks also eat many of the pond's plants, and deer come to the shores to browse the cattails, rushes, and shrubs that grow there.

These herbivores and many others transfer the energy stored in green plants into their bodies. Carnivores, animals that eat only meat, in turn eat these herbivores. For example, in the pond, larger fish eat the zooplankton and minnows that browse on the pond's vegetation. On the shore, foxes eat mice and other rodents that browse on the vegetation.

Along with the herbivores and carnivores, there are animals that eat both the vegetation and the other animals in and around the pond. These animals that eat both flesh and vegetation are called omnivores. Some of the omnivorous animals in Audubon Woods are raccoons and skunks.

As daily life progresses in the woods and pond, the animals and plants, through their life processes, make waste and die. This waste and dead material is then decomposed by other animals that are part of the detritus food chain. This is the food chain of the decomposers. Animals and plants, such as fungus, bacteria, certain worms, and certain flies, break down dead and waste material and return it to the soil as nutrients. In this manner, the resources of the ecosystem are recycled.

The delicate interrelationships of all the living and nonliving things in Audubon Woods are dependent on a balance of its natural cycles. The introduction of destructive materials, such as garbage, trash, acid rain, or other pollutants, upsets this balance and disrupts the harmony in these systems. When this happens, disastrous consequences can occur. Think of Audubon Woods as a model of our country and even the whole earth. The materials we use in everyday life can destroy the balance of the natural world.

1
Recycling:
The Issue Today

A real issue facing the people of the world today is: What do we do with all of our garbage?

My Grandma Sarah, who came to the United States from Russia, had a great philosophy—NEVER THROW ANYTHING AWAY. Everything had a use as long as a spark of life was left in it. So Grandma Sarah mended all the family clothing, including old socks. She saved the dog hair and chicken feathers to stuff pillows and comforters. Old and worn-out clothing was cut up for patches and for quilts. Kitchen wastes were composted and used in the garden and on the lawn. Grandma Sarah had the finest lawn and the largest tomatoes in the neighborhood.

Life was simpler in Grandma Sarah's time. She didn't have to contend with cardboards, plastics, and chemicals.

Most products came to her in glass containers, which she would wash and reuse or recycle back to the company. But today, if she were still alive, I know Grandma Sarah would recycle. Her motto was: Why throw something away if it's still useful?

Grandma Sarah did not know it, but she was setting a good example for the generation of the 1990s. She did what she did to save money. She also believed it was a sin to waste anything. I cannot count the number of times I heard her say, "Eat all your food, Martin, the children in Europe are starving."

What my food had to do with the children of Europe I never did figure out, but I did what she said because I respected her. Little did I know then that she was instilling in me a value that would prove absolutely necessary for the future of the planet Earth.

If all the people of the world today would put my Grandma Sarah's waste-not philosophy to work, we would have much less of a solid waste problem.

Nowadays, because of our past forty years with a throw-away attitude, the world has a garbage crisis. Now we must all waste-not. Perhaps our motivation is not the same as Grandma Sarah's, but we must do what she did so our planet will survive. It is hard work, but most things worthwhile are hard work, and more than that, Grandma Sarah's philosophy just makes good sense.

The garbage crisis today is as serious as any other environmental problem. Something must be done about this ecological hazard soon. All the trash of the earth must go somewhere. But where?

This pile of accumulated garbage represents only a very small fraction of the amount of waste we throw away every day all across this country. We must work hard to change our "throw-away" attitudes.

Each day people of the industrialized world throw out everything from paper to toothpicks to old refrigerators. Americans throw away more garbage than anyone else on earth, twice as much as Europeans do. On average, every American throws out seven and one-half pounds of garbage per day.

How do we do this? It's easy. Wake up in the morning and brush your teeth. The old toothpaste tube is empty, so toss it in the waste basket and get another. Rinse your mouth and toss the paper cup. Clean your ears with cotton swabs and then throw them away. At breakfast, have your cereal and trash the single serving box or have fruit juice in a styrofoam cup and toast on a paper plate. There is no time for washing dishes.

At school, throw out paper, paper clips, and old staples. Then go to lunch at a fast food restaurant, with all of its paper and styrofoam containers. After school, go home, have a soda, and toss the can. Perhaps make some microwave popcorn, and then out goes the bag.

For dinner, it's canned vegetables, chicken that has been wrapped in plastic and styrofoam, and more soda or another beverage that comes in a can, plastic, or bottle. Before bed, clean up and throw away the rest of the cans, bags, and food wastes. Pleasant dreams! Grandma Sarah would be shocked.

Most of this garbage (solid waste) ends up in landfills, where it is dumped, compacted, and covered with soil. The problem today is that we are running out of landfill space. Soon there will be no place to dump our garbage.

2
What Is the Solid Waste Problem?

Solid waste includes all the solid and semisolid wastes, including garbage, trash, ashes, yard wastes, swill, industrial wastes, demolition and construction wastes, and household discards, such as furniture, appliances, and other equipment.

On average, every person throws out approximately seven and one-half pounds of solid waste per day. The people of the United States alone throw out approximately 660 billion pounds of solid waste per year. This is enough solid waste to fill a four-lane highway from New York to Los Angeles six feet deep.

Most of this solid waste ends up in landfills. Because of this, we have a two-fold problem: We are wasting (unwisely using up) our natural resources; and we are taking up valuable land space for landfills that could be used for agriculture, wilderness, or communities.

Where Does the Solid Waste Come From?

Solid waste comes from the activities of people. In traditional societies (nonindustrialized), most of the wastes are natural and are given back to the environment to become part of the cycle of nature. In modern industrial societies, however, the wastes are not part of the natural cycle, and their disposal, more often than not, disrupts this cycle and is harmful to it.

In the United States, a breakdown of the nation's garbage would look like this: paper and paperboard, 40 percent; food and yard wastes, 25 percent; metals, 8.5 percent; plastics, 8 percent; glass, 7 percent; and other wastes, 11.5 percent.

Society, in general, is a giant machine that generates solid waste. In New York City, 7.2 million people generate 26,000 tons of solid waste per day. This waste comes from their homes, schools, industries, power generation plants, government offices and facilities, businesses, and recreation.

What Does Solid Waste Consist Of?

Solid waste is a reflection of the many varied activities of people. As human beings live their daily lives, they generate this waste. This waste breaks down into several categories:

Paper. This includes office and school paper, mixed paper, newspaper, and cardboard. Annually in the United

States, approximately 3.75 billion tons of paper are discarded. This equals one billion trees a year.

Metals. Thirty billion steel cans and 750 billion aluminum cans are used yearly.

Glass. Glass comes from beer bottles, soda bottles, food jars, light bulbs, buildings, and automobiles. Each year over forty-five billion tons of clear and colored glass are disposed of in the United States.

Plastics. The spectrum of plastics used in the United States is as varied as the products out in the market place. It seems that today almost everything is made of or comes wrapped in plastic. The problem with plastics is that they break down much more slowly than other waste items in a landfill. Because they degrade so slowly, they can be hazardous to wildlife, especially if they get into aquatic ecosystems. The various types of plastics are:

- *PET* (polyethylene terephthalate). PET is a common plastic used in soft drink bottles, fiberfill, boil-in bags, and carpet backing.

- *Polystyrene foam* (styrofoam). This product is common in foam cups, sandwich and salad packaging, other packaging, and insulation boards.

- *PVC* (polyvinyl chloride). This product, which is thick and transparent, is used in packaging ketchup, salad dressings, and similar products. It is also used, in a thinner malleable form, as plastic wrap.

This supermarket display of disposable plastic cups and plates, all wrapped in their own plastic packaging, is just the tip of the iceberg. Plastics may be more convenient in the short term but, over the long run, we are realizing we have less and less space for products like these that don't break down.

- *LDPE* (low-density polyethylene). LDPE is common in milk bottles, dark bottoms of soda bottles, soap bottles, and translucent plastic cups. Although damaging, this material is not as harmful to the environment as the first three plastics listed in this section.

- *Tires, food, and yard wastes.* In the United States, approximately 200 million tires are discarded annually, and 50 billion pounds of food and yard wastes are generated each year.

How Do We Cope with All of This Garbage?

Recycling offers an acceptable alternative to being buried alive in our trash. According to Natural Solid Waste Management Corporation, about 13 percent of municipal waste was recycled in 1988. Today, the techniques for recycling steel, aluminum, glass, paper, rubber, yard wastes, and plastics are well in place. The challenge will be to get people and communities motivated to use these facilities and recycle.

Thirty-eight states are now involved in promoting recycling by buying and using products that contain recycled material. Seventeen of these states also offer tax incentives to recycle. The state of Wisconsin, for example, now requires that plastic containers consist of at least 10 percent recycled paper.

3
Reduce and Reuse

All living creatures, including human beings, evolved on this planet as an integral part of its ecological systems. In early times, the first people were totally involved in the earth: They took from nature and gave back to nature. People received food and shelter from the earth and returned nutrients from their body wastes back to the environment.

With the coming of the Industrial Revolution in the late eighteenth century, great changes began to occur. Due to modern medicine and more sanitary living conditions, people began to live longer. The Industrial Revolution caused a change in the relationship between people and the earth. People began taking from the earth in a harmful fashion. They gave little, if anything good back, and the earth was slowly being destroyed.

People falsely believed that the benefits of nature were infinite (would never run out) and were put here for people alone. Even after it was discovered that the environment was finite (limited), humans continued to behave as if the earth's resources would last forever.

Instead of understanding that people had the responsibility of being the caretakers of the earth, they believed the earth would take care of itself and them. Eventually an attitude developed among humans that they were special and unique—no longer part of the natural order, but separate from it, and not dependent upon the balance of nature. This was a grave mistake.

Because of this attitude, we have created on this planet an environmental crisis that now threatens the existence of all living things, including ourselves. We have polluted the air, water, and soil, and have created mounds of solid waste that, if not controlled, will literally smother the earth.

We have now reached the point of decision. Scientists, consumer organizations, sensitive citizens, and environmental groups have made us aware of what we have been doing to the earth. The choice is ours. Should we continue as we always have, ignoring the warnings and relying on technology to save us and the planet, or should we change our behavior and start to do something positive to ensure the future of life on earth?

The answer should be obvious. We must change. But where do we begin, and how should we go about this change? There must be a new attitude developed toward the quality of our air, water, and land. In this book, we will search for answers to the solid waste problems.

What can be done to alleviate the garbage crisis in the world today? The answer lies in the four R's:

1. *Reduce* the amount of waste produced

2. *Reuse* items instead of throwing them out

3. *Recycle* waste materials

4. *Recover* energy from waste

Reducing the Amount of Waste Produced

The first step in reducing the amount of waste people generate is to make people aware of the fact that all of our products, including the energy used to make and run them, come from natural resources.

A natural resource is any substance that occurs naturally in nature, that is, forests, air, water, minerals, fossil fuels, and so forth. There are two types of natural resources: renewable and nonrenewable. A renewable resource is any resource that can be derived from an endless or cyclical source. It is constantly being replenished. A nonrenewable resource is any substance only available in limited amounts. These substances may take millions of years to develop and, therefore, they are nonreplenishable.

From the beginning of human existence in societies, as previously stated, people believed that the benefits of nature would always be there for them. This belief established a

This sign pointing to the local recycling center serves as a reminder that recycling is one very important step in the 4-step process of alleviating our garbage crisis.

pattern of behavior that I refer to as use and abuse: Use whatever you can and abuse what's left. This pattern continued for thousands of years, eventually leaving people in a world rapidly running out of the very resources that sustained them. However, the use and abuse pattern still continued because people believed that their technology (the application of science to industry) would save them. If a certain resource was depleted, then new technology would find a way to do the same functions with different resources. For example, today we have an energy crisis but, instead of reducing the amount of energy being consumed, people are using up our energy sources as fast as ever. They believe that new technology will find a way to use alternative energy sources so they can continue to do exactly as they have been doing.

There are two problems with this attitude: One, new technology may not provide the answer; and, two, our technologies, besides making life more comfortable for us, have also created new problems as well as answers. New technologies create new chemicals and pollutants with which we must deal. Sometimes these new pollutants are not even discovered until after they have done irreparable damage to the environment.

New technologies have created billions of tons of packaging and other materials that must be disposed of. This has been technology's mark on the world—it has made us the generation that generates more garbage than any in the history of people. Thus, besides using up our

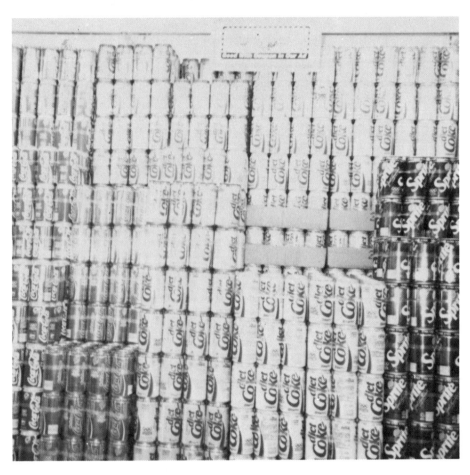

This display of soft drinks, packaged in aluminum cans held together by plastic rings, reminds us that just about everything we purchase comes in packaging we must somehow dispose of.

natural resources, we are throwing what's left out in our garbage.

In the United States, we discard enough office paper each year to construct a 12-foot-high wall from Los Angeles to New York City. We dispose of enough glass bottles to fill both the Sears Tower and John Hancock Building in Chicago every two weeks. We go through 2.5 million plastic containers per hour. We waste 9 percent of the edible food we purchase. We trash 18 billion disposable diapers each year. We generate enough garbage each year to fill 65,000 garbage trucks. These trucks, if put end-to-end, would form a line that would reach halfway from the earth to the moon.

What Communities Are Doing

Before we become buried alive in our own garbage, something must be done to stop this garbage glut. This crisis has finally made Americans realize that the garbage they generate must go somewhere. As a result, many states and communities have embarked on waste-reduction programs that will reduce the amount of waste generated and will recycle what can be recycled. In July of 1990, Minneapolis and St. Paul, Minnesota, banned all plastic food packaging that will not degrade or cannot be recycled. In 1993, Nebraska put a ban on most disposable diapers. Most communities now have mandatory recycling laws that require residents to separate their glass, paper, aluminum cans, steel cans, and plastics from the rest of their garbage.

This community bin contains steel cans to be recycled. Recycling containers, like steel cans, helps make the problems of excess packaging more manageable.

This will help reduce the amount of garbage being generated by communities.

What You Can Do

Twelve-year-old Mary Robinson was worried about the environment. Her teacher had told Mary's class that the world is in an environmental crisis. He had said that one of the main problems is all the garbage being generated in the United States. This really bothered Mary, so she asked her teacher if she could do a project on reducing waste and reusing materials.

Mary wanted to convince her classmates and her parents that reducing waste is important, and that it is every person's responsibility to reduce waste and reuse materials. The first thing Mary did was read all the literature she could find on the garbage crisis. She wrote to her state's Department of Natural Resources, which sent her information on the subject.

After researching the problem, Mary then compiled a list of things that people could do to reduce waste and reuse materials:

To Reduce Waste

1. Examine what you buy, and purchase fewer materials that quickly become waste. Read the labels of these materials to see if they can be safely reused.

2. Take care of materials you buy so they will last longer. As an example, if you properly grease and maintain your bicycle, it will last for years.

3. Use returnable beverage bottles. When you return these bottles, the company sterilizes them and refills them with the same product to be sold again.

4. Bring home groceries in the fewest number of bags possible. Use paper bags and then reuse them for other purposes, such as recycling newspaper or for garbage. If possible, shop with cloth bags. These bags will reduce the devastation of our trees, a valuable natural resource.

5. Buy food and other products in the least amount of packaging possible. Buy bulk products instead of prepackaged materials.

6. Refuse to buy products wrapped or served in foam or plastic. This type of pressure, put on chain restaurants and stores, can make them change their practices. Just recently, one large restaurant chain moved away from using styrofoam wrapping to paper. They did this because of consumer pressure.

7. Avoid throw-away products. Instead of paper, use cloth dishtowels, napkins, and rags. Use glass or ceramic dishes instead of styrofoam, plastic, or paper.

8. Use cloth diapers instead of disposable diapers. A cloth diaper an be reused over and over.

9. Buy products made of recycled materials or materials that can be recycled. This will reduce the depletion of our natural resources.

To Reuse Materials

1. Reuse all the materials you own as much as possible by finding new and innovative uses for these materials. Bottles can be used for storing pins, buttons, and other items. A plastic milk bottle can be used as a watering pitcher or a planter. When filled with stones and recapped, the plastic milk bottle makes a great anchor.

2. Save the oil from the family car and take it to the nearest collection facility so it can be reprocessed and used again.

3. Most kitchen scraps (coffee grounds, potato peelings, eggshells, melon rinds, etc.) make a wonderful addition to a compost heap.

4. Start a compost heap in your yard, and use your yard and kitchen wastes to make a valuable soil conditioner for your lawn or garden.

5. Wide-mouthed glass or plastic jars make great storage bins for nuts and bolts and other household items.

Her lists composed, Mary presented her report to the class. She gave each of her classmates a copy of the list and encouraged them to do as much as possible to see that the items on the list were implemented.

After giving her report to the class, Mary and several of her classmates formed a committee and went to the school principal. They asked the principal to have the school implement a program that would utilize the recommendations on Mary's list.

If you follow Mary's suggestions and urge others to do so also, helping save natural resources and reducing the garbage glut will eventually spread throughout your community. From your community, it will spread to your state and, from your state, to the nation. Perhaps a whole new attitude among people will develop, and we will become the waste-not generation.

Reuse

By reusing items, you can reduce the amount of garbage you generate and save money in the process. Reuse is the most efficient form of recycling, requiring no new natural resources or energy. It helps preserve the environment by reducing pollution of the air, water, and land.

Even recycling uses energy. Any time fuel is used in the manufacturing process, valuable energy supplies are being dwindled away. The use of energy also means that a certain amount of air pollution is occurring. Any time fuel is burned in the manufacturing process, exhaust fumes and particles are emitted through the smokestacks of the industries into the atmosphere. These gases and particles add to our air pollution woes. It makes sense, therefore, to reduce

The exhaust fumes and particles pouring out of these smokestacks are the result of energy being produced. Therefore, if we can use less energy by recycling, instead of producing materials from scratch, we can limit the amount of pollution released into our air.

the amount of manufacturing. We can do this by reusing products.

Reusing products also reduces the demand for raw materials. Natural resources, such as forests, minerals, and energy supplies, will last much longer if we reuse items instead of throwing them away.

Ways to Conserve

The way to implement Mary's list and to add to it is to purchase items that are made to be used many times, items such as cloth diapers, cloth napkins, cloth towels, cloth rags, sponges, china or earthenware dishes, silverware, rechargeable batteries, glass soda bottles that the company sterilizes and refills, mechanical pencils, fountain pens, and so forth.

Use both sides of a sheet of paper. Scrap paper should be saved and used for notes or grocery lists. Repair appliances instead of purchasing new ones. Mend clothing. Use cloth grocery bags. Purchase many of your items at second-hand stores or junk yards. Buy used cars. Encourage local industry to reuse materials in the manufacture of their products.

Most importantly, like Mary, encourage your friends, teachers, parents, and relatives to reuse their items. If we can get many people to do this, it will make a big difference in the amount of items that need to be produced.

The Diaper Dilemma

Each week, in the United States, millions of diapers are used. It is estimated that an average of eighty-five disposable diapers per child are used per week. That's a lot of diapers. Using disposable diapers consumes more raw materials, water, and energy than reusable cloth diapers. More air pollution is created in producing disposable diapers, and much more waste pollution is created through their use.

It would appear that the answer to the disposable diaper problem would be to get people not to use them, but this is a difficult task. Disposable diapers are convenient, keep babies drier and more comfortable, and are much less work for the parents. Cloth diapers must be washed and smell strongly of ammonia. This smell, as they sit in the laundry room, can permeate the entire house. Diaper services are expensive.

There is some evidence, however, that the washing of reusable cloth diapers is also harmful to the environment. The chemicals accumulated in the diaper go directly into the sewers, which wind up in our water supply.

So where's the answer? Proctor & Gamble, the nation's largest disposable diaper-maker, is spending large amounts of money to research the problem and fund recycling projects. One of these research projects, in Seattle, Washington, will collect used diapers from 1,000 volunteer households. The diapers will be washed and sanitized before being separated into plastic and pulp. The plastic will be recycled into flower pots, garbage bags, and park benches. The pulp will be used in cardboard boxes, building insulation, and wallboard liner.

What to Do with Other Plastics

Plastics were mentioned earlier in this book. Many of these materials do not degrade (break down) readily, and they harm the environment by releasing toxins into the natural systems. Knowing this, the question is, Should we or should we not use degradable plastics?

With today's technology, there are two kinds of degradable plastics: photodegradable and biodegradable. Photodegradable plastic breaks down when exposed to ultraviolet radiation. Biodegradable plastic breaks down via the action of microorganisms in the detritus food chain (decomposition).

By using degradable plastics, we reinforce the throwaway mentality of the nation that got us into this garbage dilemma. Degradables also lessen the efforts to recycle plastics that are able to be recycled. Also, little is known about what kind of impact the residues of these degradable plastics will have on the water systems and soil once they start to break down.

Today, recycling plastics is the most reliable and safest way to deal with plastic wastes. Recycling plastics reduces the stress on our landfills, saves energy and natural resources, and provides materials that can be used in other plastic products.

4
Recover and Recycle

Recovering Energy

Energy is the ability to do work. Without energy, life on earth could not exist. Ninety-five percent of the world's energy comes from the sun. The other 5 percent comes from geothermal (pressures within the earth itself) or nuclear (from the nucleus of atoms) sources.

Light, the energy from the sun, is an infinite source of energy. This means that it will not run out. Nature uses this light energy to carry on all of its functions, including transferring this light energy into other forms of energy. These other forms of energy are finite (limited) and, once used up, are irreplaceable.

Besides the garbage crisis, today we also have an energy crisis. The major energy sources for people in the modern, industrialized world are coal, oil, and natural gas. These are fossil fuels—fuels derived from the remains of plants and animals. It takes millions of years for fossil fuels to be formed. This is why these energy sources are referred to as nonrenewable resources. Once used up, they cannot be replaced.

Today, at the present rates of consumption, it is estimated the world has approximately a 30-year supply of oil, a 25-year supply of natural gas, and a 500-year supply of coal. It is possible that, in our lifetimes, the world may run out of some kinds of fossil fuel energy.

Recovering energy from our waste may help alleviate this impending crisis. Burning garbage appears to be an attractive alternative to landfills because it reduces, by as much as 90 percent, the volume of waste that must be buried. The energy produced from burning can be used to heat water to turn generators to make electricity and, thus, reduce our dependence on fossil fuels. Plastics, when burned, generate as much energy as fuel oil. However, incineration of trash is a very controversial issue because of the many problems attached to the process. If not built and operated properly, these incinerators release toxic air pollutants, such as dioxins.

Today, the debate continues. People in favor of incineration argue that the benefits far outweigh the negatives. They point out that all forms of waste reduction, including landfills and recycling, are energy-users. For example, to run an average landfill, 43,000 gallons of fuel are used per week—30,000 gallons are used in collection and 13,000 gallons in the landfilling process itself. Recycling saves, but it still unnecessarily uses energy. Incineration produces energy.

This oil well serves as a reminder of our dependence on fossil fuels, like petroleum. With our reserves dwindling ever so quickly, we are faced with the possibility of running out of petroleum, as a fuel energy, in our lifetime.

Proponents of incineration also argue that new pollution controls, such as high-temperature furnaces, scrubbers, and bag houses installed in these facilities, eliminate most of the harmful air pollution emissions. Japan has built over 300 waste-to-energy plants, in which 40 percent of the country's wastes are burned and an estimated 35 percent recycled.

People against incineration argue that the emissions contain cancer-causing substances, such as mercury, dioxins, and ash. As this issue continues to make controversy, it is wise to concentrate our efforts on recycling as both an energy-saving and garbage-reduction method.

Recycling

Recycling makes good sense for people. It is not a new process. It has been around ever since the beginning of life on earth. The earth, you see, could not exist without the recycling process. Nature recycles everything. This is how our planet constantly renews itself.

It was not until the development of technology and the Industrial Revolution that people moved away from these natural processes. With technology came the idea that people were not part of nature, that we were separate and distinct. This thinking is what brought us to the environmental crisis we are now experiencing.

Like all other organisms on earth, people, too, are part of the natural cycles of nature. Instead of disrupting these cycles, we should be enhancing them. They are the very source of our existence.

Incinerators like this one are at the center of much controversy today. While they present one option for dealing with over-crowded landfills, there are many problems associated with their use.

5
People Recycling

Mary Robinson was so successful with her project on reduce and reuse, that her teacher, Mr. Gutnik, decided to do a class project on recycling. Mr. Gutnik reminded the class that, like nature, people must learn not to waste natural resources. He told the class that recycling is the process of reprocessing and using products over again.

The class was divided into several different groups. One group was assigned to research the question: Why recycle? A second group was to research the recycling of aluminum and other metals and report back to the class. A third group was to research recycling paper; and, finally, the fourth group was to report on yard and kitchen waste recycling. Each group was given one month to complete its project and then report back to the class.

Why Recycle?

Ben Rissin chaired the group that considered reasons to recycle. He and his group stood before the class while they presented their report. Ben started out by stating the problem. In all science projects, the problem must be defined before you can do anything about it.

The problem, as Ben explained it, is that most of the nation's garbage ends up in landfills. A landfill is a place where waste is dumped, compacted, and covered over with soil. These landfills take up valuable space, creating a land use dilemma.

Ben then explained to the class that, after his group defined the problem, they researched the idea in order to make observations about the issue. All scientific investigations must start with observations on the problem.

Millie Waxman, one of the members of the group, then explained that, according to their group's research, in an average state, like Wisconsin, anywhere from 14,000 to 20,000 acres of land are used for landfills. She further explained that 70 to 100 average-sized farms could operate on this same acreage. However, the land is being used for garbage, not agriculture. In a world where food is scarce, this does not seem right.

Emily Heiser, also a member of the group, told the class that, in the process of doing the project, group members took the information they had gathered and classified it into groups. She reported on how landfills can also cause water pollution and produce hazardous gases.

Emily explained that, as rain or melting snow seeps through the buried trash, a leachate (contaminated water drained from soil) is formed. This water can poison the ground and surface water. She told the class that it is not uncommon for a hazardous leachate to form from landfills.

Emily further explained that hazardous gases, such as methane, can also be formed in landfills. These gases come from the decomposition of food wastes and yard wastes. Some of these gases are also formed from the decomposition of plastics. Decomposition of plastics produces such gases as vinyl chloride and hydrogen sulfide. All of these gases are very dangerous to living things.

Ben told the class that landfills are also very expensive to build and operate. As land becomes more scarce, the costs rise rapidly, and the taxpayers are the ones who must pay the bill.

With all these negatives, Ben's group came up with the inference (an inference is an educated guess based upon what you have observed) that it just makes good sense to reduce the amount of landfill space needed by recycling items instead of trashing them.

The group put their inference into a hypothesis (a statement that can be tested). They said: Recycling will save landfill space, energy, natural resources, and money.

Ben went on to explain that his group tested this hypothesis by researching the benefits of present recycling programs in their community. They discovered that recycling a ton of newspapers saves approximately 17 trees, conserves the energy needed to cut these trees down, and earned the recycler money when he or she sold the papers.

The group discovered that items that can easily be recycled are paper, aluminum and steel cans, and glass. Plastics, too, can be recycled, but it is a bit more difficult.

The way for you, as an individual, to recycle is to set up a recycling area in your home. This area should have separate containers for aluminum cans, steel cans, glass, plastics, and newspapers. Find out if your community has curbside recycling or if you must take the materials to your community's recycling center. Today, most communities have recycling centers.

Ben told the class that his group concluded that, if a person recycled products in his or her home and if a community recycled products in its institutions (such as schools, hospitals, government offices, etc.), we would all be doing our parts to reduce the garbage crisis.

Furthermore, Ben continued, if one community recycles, the idea will spread to other communities. Soon an entire state will be recycling. From one state, the word will spread to other states. Then these states will set up recycling programs. Eventually the entire nation will be recycling. Once the nation recycles, the practice may spread to other countries. Finally, the practice of recycling will spread from country to country until the entire world will be recycling.

Recycling newspapers like these can help save our trees for future generations of animals to build habitats in and people to enjoy.

Recycling Aluminum and Other Metals

Over the years my students in my science classes have done a number of environmental studies. Below are just a few. Mario Moffet, chairperson of the group that studied metal recycling, stood before the class. He stated that his group, in its research, discovered that Environmental Protection Agency (EPA) studies have shown that the use of recycled materials to make products, almost always reduces the environmental impact of manufacturing goods from virgin materials. Energy is saved whenever goods are recycled. The energy savings alone makes recycling worthwhile. And the benefits of recycling far outweigh any inconvenience that people experience by separating their garbage and dropping it at the recycling center.

Anne Kramer, a girl in Mario's group, explained that, in their project, they found out that the energy savings was really tremendous if you recycle. For example, she told the class that a ton of coal is saved when recycling one ton of iron, instead of processing one ton of virgin iron. The amount of water used in recycling iron is 40 percent less than the amount of water used in processing virgin iron, water pollution is 75 percent less, and air pollution is 86 percent less. There is a 97 percent energy savings by recycling iron.

It is also the same for aluminum, Anne continued. Aluminum recycling reduces water pollution by 97 percent, and air pollution by 95 percent, and saves approximately 95 percent of the energy used in the original manufacturing process. When one ton of aluminum is recycled, it saves the equivalent of 2,350 gallons of gasoline. This is equal to the energy used by a typical midwestern home over a period of ten years. Anne stated that, according to her figures, it was a puzzle to her as to why there should even be a question about recycling.

Andy Sumner was responsible for reporting on how to actually recycle aluminum and steel cans. He stated that the process of recycling in your home is almost the same for both aluminum and steel cans. First, rinse all cans and flatten the aluminum cans. Aluminum cans are easily flattened. You can even buy can flatteners at department or hardware stores. Steel cans are harder to flatten. It would probably be better if you did not try to flatten them.

Next, put the cans in a recycling bin in your garage or basement. When the bin gets full, take the cans to a recycling center or to a scrap dealer.

Aluminum is manufactured from bauxite. Researchers in the industry have discovered that making new aluminum from bauxite is ten times more expensive than reprocessing used cans. Because it is less expensive to reuse aluminum and steel, your cans are worth money. The dealer will buy them from you.

Andy went on to say that both aluminum and steel are reprocessed into many different products, including more cans, sheet metal, doors, windows, and house siding.

Mario told the class that, from its research, his group concluded that it was both logical and practical to recycle

This bin is full of steel cans, waiting to be processed for recycling. Unlike aluminum cans, that are easy to flatten, it is best not to try to flatten steel cans.

aluminum and other metals because recycling would save money, energy, and natural resources.

Recycling Paper

Angela Croysdale, leader of the third group, put recycled paper, which her group had made, on a table in front of the class. Then she spoke to the class, and told them that each year Americans use over 67 million tons of paper (600 pounds per person). The United States is the largest consumer of paper in the world. Just within the last 25 years, paper consumption in this country has doubled and, with the popularity of computers, will continue to rise. Most of this paper ends up in landfills.

Angela continued to say that it is important that we recycle as much waste as possible. Recycled paper is made from waste paper pulp instead of trees. Newspapers can be made into newsprint and other low grade paper. Clean office paper or school paper is recycled into the same type of quality paper as before, and can be reused by offices and schools.

Tara Baker, Angela's co-chairperson, explained how their group recycled paper. The group took old newspapers and soaked them in a solution of vinegar and water. After allowing the papers to soak for one day, they removed the papers from that solution and drained them over a sink. The paper was then put into another solution of plain water. After soaking for an hour, the paper was beaten with an electric mixer until it became a mushy pulp. Once it became pulpy enough, it was removed from the water and placed on framed screens. The pulp was then rolled with a rolling pin, and the excess water was drained into a sink. The pulp was made as thin as possible. Afterwards, it was removed from the screen and ironed.

Tara held up a piece of the recycled paper her group had made. "This is the result of our efforts," she said. Tara then showed the class the group's report, which was written on the recycled paper they had made.

Dane Johnson, another member of Angela's group, told the class more about recycling paper. He said the National Association of Recycling Industries estimates that over 200 million trees are saved each year due to current recycling efforts. Paper products consume approximately 35 percent of the world's annual commercial wood harvest. This, he continued, is expected to increase to 50 percent by the year 2,000, due to the demand for more paper, especially for computers.

Angela spoke to the class again. Recycling paper is one of the easier recycling processes, and use of the process is increasing, but not fast enough to keep up with paper consumption. Many companies are now using recycled paper. Some greeting card companies print their cards on recycled paper. Some restaurants package their products in recycled paper. There are more uses, but not enough.

In 1965, 20 percent of all paper products in the United States were recycled. By 1980, that figure had increased only to 24 percent. Recycling must increase at a much greater rate if we are to preserve our forests.

It makes sense to recycle paper. The quality of recycled paper is equal to the paper manufactured from virgin pulp. Quite often recycled paper possesses qualities that make it even more desirable than paper made from virgin pulp.

Angela held up a piece of the paper her group had made. It was more opaque, dense, and flexible than non-recycled paper.

Angela set the recycled paper down. From her group's research, she continued, the group concluded that recycling paper could be an economic boon to the nation. It creates new material resources, reduces the tax burden, and reduces pollution and energy consumption. Recycling paper creates many new jobs. It provides more jobs than the actual harvesting and manufacturing of virgin pulp paper.

Recycling Yard and Kitchen Wastes

The fourth group, led by Matt Kruger, presented its report. Matt said that 17 percent of all household waste is yard waste (grass clippings, leaves, plants, branches, twigs, brush, weeds, etc.). He asked the class to try to think about how much space that takes up in landfills. Add food scraps to that 17 percent, and you come up with 20 percent of the total household waste stream. That's a lot of garbage to go into landfills.

Dmitry Bikovsky, a member of Matt's group, explained that yard wastes and food scraps don't have to be part of the landfill problem. They can be recycled, naturally, back into the environment through composting. He further explained that the word "composting" comes from the Latin word meaning "to put together." In composting, the yard wastes and food scraps are mixed with other materials in a compost heap. This heap allows these biodegradable organic wastes to be recycled naturally. Composting, in fact, sets up desirable conditions for decomposition to take place.

"Our group built a compost heap," Matt said as he took over again. He turned on a video presentation, and the class watched part of his group raking leaves and collecting grass clippings. Others were collecting kitchen scraps and, temporarily, putting them into plastic containers.

Matt narrated. "We learned in class that decomposition is essential in the cycle of life because it frees carbon, nitrogen, and other nutrients from the decomposing materials so that they can find their way back into the life stream."

A picture flashed on the screen showing the materials Matt's group would use to build the composting area. There were tools of various sorts, ready-mix concrete, snow fencing, fence posts, the yard wastes, the kitchen scraps, lime, a large thermometer, a pitchfork, and a long wooden dowel.

This community compost heap is far larger than an individual family's might be. But, compost heaps serve the same purpose, whether they are right in your own backyard or on community property.

A compost heap, Matt continued, is really a busy complex of organic material decomposing organic wastes. The pile relies upon microbes as its workhorses. Microbes are tiny plants and animals that aid in the process of decomposition. Microbes are not the only organisms in a compost pile. Earthworms and insects are also part of this decomposition process but, because there are so many more microbes and because they are such efficient decomposers, microbes decompose material much faster than worms and insects.

Microbes are organisms, such as bacteria, molds, yeasts, and protozoans (one-celled animals). These microbes exist in colonies consisting of millions of these tiny organisms. They digest and oxidize garbage, which creates a good rich humus, which, when mixed with soil, increases the soil's fertility (ability to support life-producing organisms).

Jessica Volpe continued the report. She told the class that her group's project was based upon the inference: Composting will reduce the amount of garbage generated by a household.

Matt's group decided to put its compost heap in an area in a sunny spot, but out of the way so it wouldn't interfere with the family's outdoor activities. The heap was five feet square, with a turning bin five feet square next to it. A turning bin is an additional area in which the compost pile is turned.

Matt's group removed all the grass from the area they had chosen and measured. Jessica explained: It is important, in order for the compost pile to function properly, that it have direct contact with the soil. This allows for microbes in the soil to enter the compost heap.

Holes were dug, and fence posts were put in the ground. After the posts were in place, the snow fence was wired to the posts. Matt's group laid brush and wood chips, three to four inches deep, over the fenced-in area. Jessica explained that this base allowed for excellent drainage and good air circulation throughout the pile. Next, the group layered the heap. They put six to eight inches of kitchen scraps over the base and watered it down. They then layered one inch of yard soil mixed with lime over the kitchen scraps. This layer provides the nitrogen needed by the microbes that enter the pile from the yard soil. This layer should be kept damp.

The layering process was repeated until the pile was about three feet high, and then the top was covered with straw. Jessica explained that the straw prevented rain from washing away the nutrients in the pile.

Joey Luther said that the group allowed the heap to stand for a week and then checked its temperature. The temperature, he explained, should be at 60°C to 71°C (140°F to 160°F) in order for the heap to work properly.

He further explained that the group would allow the heap to stand for six weeks and then they would turn it. This is done by forking the heap into a new pile in the turning bin. After the new pile is formed, it should be moistened and covered with straw. This process would be repeated every few weeks. In four months, by spring, the compost would be ready to mix in with garden and flower beds.

Matt stood again. He explained that the group monitored the household garbage throughout the entire project. From the results, the group concluded that composting prevents a significant amount of garbage from entering the waste stream.

He went on to tell the class that composting is something you can do as an individual to reduce the waste stream. It doesn't matter whether your pile is small or large—what you must do to compost organic material is the same.

By mixing compost you make with the soil in your yard or garden, you are returning organic matter to the soil in a usable form. This organic matter improves plant growth by loosening the soil and increasing its capacity to hold water. It also adds essential nutrients, required by plants, to the soil.

By composting, you not only reduce the amount of garbage in the waste stream, you also help eliminate the special problems that organic matter can create in a landfill. These organic wastes in landfills can produce methane gas, a gas that can explode in areas without good ventilation. Organic wastes in landfills can also create a strong leachate, a liquid that causes minerals and, sometimes, poisons to come out of the solids and become part of the liquid. This leachate then seeps into the groundwater and contaminates it.

6
Recycling
Projects for
Home and School

Perhaps one of the best ways to observe nature and discover how it works is really to become involved in the process itself. It works the same way with people and what we do. Things always seem to be better understood when we are involved in what's happening. This can be accomplished by researching and doing projects, like the class in chapter 5, that are centered around ideas you are observing or studying.

Projects with Glass

Recycling one ton of glass saves one ton of oil. Recycled glass uses 50 percent less water in its manufacture; the air pollution from glass manufacturing is reduced 20 percent by recycling; and wastes from mining silicone are reduced by 80 percent.

Glass bottles like these are used for many different types of packaging. Recycling or reusing glass bottles is an efficient way to reduce waste and conserve energy.

As anyone can see, reusing glass costs less than manufacturing new glass. If you do not reuse the glass jars and bottles in your home, they can be recycled.

PROJECT: See how much glass you can recycle in one month.

Collect all the glass used in your household every day and weigh it. Set up a recycling area for this glass. Label boxes or bins for brown, green, and clear glass. Wash the glass containers out, and remove all metal caps and rings. You do not have to remove the labels.

After one month has passed, add up the totals of the glass you have recycled. This will show you how much glass you are removing from the waste stream.

If you can, convince your class to recycle glass as a class project. Follow the same procedures as above to see how much glass your class can remove from the waste stream in a month.

Recycled glass can be melted down and made into new bottles and jars. Some of the glass will be crushed and used in roads as glassphalt, a combination of glass and asphalt.

Projects with Plastics

The plastics recycling industry is still in the early stages of development. Manufacturers, because of the nature of plastic, are still discovering how these items can be recycled. Today, only about 1 percent of the plastic manufactured is being recycled.

Plastic can be easily recycled. It is a material that lends itself to being collected, washed, chopped, and reformed under heat and pressure into new products. However, the nature of the plastic itself has prevented recycling efforts. Because plastics are made from a variety of different resins, they do not perform well when mixed together in the recycling process. They are also very bulky and take up much space. Therefore, they are expensive to collect and process for recycling.

Yet, as land fills up, it becomes apparent that plastics must be recycled. Manufacturers are now attempting to think of new and innovative uses for recycled plastics. Some of these uses are stuffing for jackets, lumber fillers, and new plastic containers made from the recycled containers.

PROJECT: *Recycle plastic for school supplies.*

By recycling plastic, you can provide your school with inexpensive, much-needed supplies. Try to get many of your classmates actively involved in the recycling process. In an effort to do this, you might create a flyer for your class that lists plastic items that can be recycled or reused in the classroom. The flyer could look something like the example on the following page.

After the plastic items have been collected, each classroom can brainstorm possible uses for the items that have been collected. Assign a certain number of items to groups of students, and have them use the items for specific projects. Any leftover materials should be recycled.

PLASTICS FOR CLASSROOMS

Teachers, Students, Parents
Join Our Effort

RECYCLE PLASTIC FOR SCHOOL

At home, wash and save the following items:

- Plastic milk bottles
- Plastic soda bottles
- Plastic yogurt containers and lids
- Margarine tubs and other plastic containers and lids
- Tops of plastic milk bottles
- Plastic shopping bags
- Plastic forks, knives, and spoons
- Plastic lids
- Styrofoam packaging materials
- Plastic trays from microwaveable prepared foods
- Plastic jars

Bring all your washed items to the gymnasium on _____, 199__, and place them in labeled bins located around the room. These items will be used by classrooms for school projects and supplies.

This example of a flyer for classroom use could be adapted for home or community recycling as well.

Some projects the class groups may make are:

1. Bird feeders from the plastic milk bottles

2. Bird houses from the plastic milk bottles

3. Paint trays from plastic trays

4. Pencil holders from plastic jars

5. A clear bottle piggy bank for younger children

6. A checker set from plastic caps

Projects with Tires

In the United States, over 250 million tires are trashed every year. New mountains are forming in this country, not geologic mountains that will eventually grow trees and have streams and lakes, but mountains of ugly discarded tires. Landfills will not take tires because they take up too much room, do not burn well, and are a fire hazard. The only thing that can be done with these tires, besides using them for playgrounds swings, planters, and borders in your yard, is to shred them.

To get rid of these mountains of tires, companies are now coming up with innovative ideas for recycling. Recycling tires, however, is not an easy job, and it is a slow process, because there are only a few facilities with the equipment to do the job.

Most old tires must first go to a shredder. The shredder eats about 800 tires an hour. It reduces the tires to two inch square bits, grinds them to a granular texture, and takes

Tires like these, discarded from automobiles and trucks, pile up, with no place to go. Landfills will not take them, because they take up too much room, and attempts at burning them create poisonous fumes.

out the metal. The rubber crumbs are sold to tire manufacturers to use in making new tires.

Besides being shredded, some other things can be done with these old, worn-out tires. Some of the tires have the tread peeled off and then are retreaded for use again. Some tires are used to make door mats, truck bed mats, boat bumpers on piers, and roads.

A company in Michigan searches for new and innovative uses for old tires. They have studied such uses as in landscaping mulch, in septic systems, and sludge to speed up composting.

Recycled tires can also be combined with other materials, such as plastic, to make sturdier products, such as hoses, piping, toys, sports fields, and road beds.

One of the most innovative uses for old tires has been accomplished by actor Dennis Weaver, who had his house built out of old tires. Three thousand of them! It is said that these tires have enough insulating quality to keep the temperatures in the house comfortable all year long.

Yet even with all this recycling, the tire mountains continue to grow. Why? Because there are far too many tires for the facilities available to recycle them. Perhaps states should give financial incentives to companies who are willing to invest in tire-shredding facilities. This would help reduce the ugly latex mountains.

PROJECT: Make a fort from old tires.

Have your classroom collect old tires (you may use a flyer, like one suggested in the plastics project). Once the tires are collected, design a fort with your teacher or parent helping. Then use the tires and build your fort.

You may also use old tires to build a playground maze. Again, a thorough design will be required before building.

Other Projects

Listed below are some projects you may want to attempt at school or at home.

- Investigate littering and the problems it can cause. Answer such questions as: How does litter add to the stream of garbage problems? Why is littering dangerous?

- Study decomposition. Attempt to understand the decomposition process. Answer a variety of questions: What is nature's role in decomposition? How does decomposition recycle nutrients? Does decomposition occur in landfills?

- Do a project on recycling paper. Answer questions: How does recycling paper save trees? Why is recycling paper important?

- Build a recycling center at school or at home. Keep a log on how the recycling center works. Answer questions: Does the recycling center make recycling easier? How does recycling reduce the garbage stream?

- Create a microbe garden in which you can study how certain microorganisms aid in the process of decomposition. Describe the microorganisms you observe by diagramming them. Tell what organic material these microorganisms appear to be decomposing.

- Build a compost pile at home or school. Study how the process of decomposition works in the pile. Observe how a rich humus develops within the pile. Answer the following questions: Why is composting important? How does compost improve the soil in your garden?

There are many more recycling projects that you can do. All of the projects will require research and study. For information on projects, write to your state department of natural resources or get science project books from the library. You may also ask your school's science teacher for some project ideas.

Benefits of Recycling

Why recycle? Recycling helps preserve our natural resources, especially the nonrenewable natural resources. By recycling, we also save valuable landfill space. This land can then be used for agriculture or wilderness areas. Recycling saves energy. By reducing the energy used, it also reduces air and water pollution. It is economical to recycle. In most cases, it costs less money to recycle products than to make new products from virgin materials. Also, recycling reduces the stream of garbage, litter, and trash. Finally, recycling will help you develop an environmental ethic. You will feel that you are playing a responsible role in preserving the natural environment for yourself and other generations to come. In order to feel like you can make a difference, you must play an active role in helping to save our environment. Recycling is one way to become actively involved.

7
What You Can Do

We all help contribute to the "garbage dilemma," because we all tend to throw things out that are still useful. However, if we precycled, recycled, and reused products, we would make the first important step to solving the problem.

Precycle

One important thing that you can do as an individual is to reduce the garbage stream before it starts. You can do this by yourself and convince others to precycle. Shop wisely and avoid waste. Refuse to buy food served in or on foam or plastic. If you are having a picnic or party and think you must use throwaway items, use paper products instead of plastics. The paper will degrade in a landfill, whereas plastics will not.

If you have little brothers or sisters or nieces and nephews, convince your parents and aunts and uncles to use cloth diapers, not paper. Every year Americans throw away 18 billion disposable diapers. These diapers take up valuable landfill space and take approximately 500 years to decompose.

Packaging of food and other products is a real contributor to the garbage crisis. Americans spend one-tenth of their grocery budgets on packaging.

Each American uses about 60 pounds of packaging per year. This packaging is usually discarded, to become part of the waste stream, as soon as the package is opened. A great deal of this packaging is made of plastic that will not decompose easily in landfills. Packaging accounts for approximately one-third of all the garbage we send to landfills.

Avoid Waste

Most people, as a result of being consumers and users of goods and services in today's world, produce some waste. But there are ways to avoid being an environmentally unsound consumer. You can think about what you consume, research how it is made, and, if the product is not good for the environment, find an alternative that is. Ask yourself the following questions: In what ways do the items I am purchasing contribute to the garbage stream? How can I purchase and dispose of items to generate less garbage?

You could buy goods in returnable or recyclable containers. This would reduce your throwaways and, therefore, reduce the trash you generate.

Packages like these bags of chips look harmless enough sitting on the shelf. But, when you stop to realize that each bag that is purchased must eventually be discarded, and multiply these two tiny shelves by all of the products in a supermarket, that's a lot of packaging to dispose of.

If you purchase recyclables, you must discover where to take them so that they can be recycled properly. It does no good for you to recycle so someone else can throw the items out.

You should avoid using styrofoam or plastic products. The manufacturing process for these products is often not good for the environment, and these products, due to their nature, do not decompose for hundreds of years. They do, however, fill up landfill sites and take up valuable land space.

Be responsible with leftover foods and yard wastes. Start a compost pile in your backyard and urge others to do the same. By composting, you reduce the garbage stream a great deal. You are also giving something back to the environment instead of constantly taking away.

Become an environmental activist. Join other people who are interested in reducing waste and preserving the environment. Speak out about your concerns for the environment. Encourage environmentally responsible policies by supporting government officials who are pro-ecology. Back the global ecological movement to improve the ecology of the planet.

Epilogue

With each passing year, we find ourselves more involved in environmental crises that we create. As this book demonstrates, today we are buried deep in our own garbage problems. We have tried to resolve some of these problems, but, as of yet, we have barely made a dent.

Just what is the problem we are facing today? In a world that is overpopulated with people, it is becoming more obvious to many experts that all of our environmental problems, including our garbage problems, stem from too many people using too much of the earth's resources too fast. The earth can only support so much life. When there is too much life in any area, that area becomes stressed because it is operating over its carrying capacity. Carrying capacity is how much life any given area of the earth can support.

On almost all fronts, masses of people are stretching the earth's ecosystems to the point of collapse. One immediate step that must be taken, in order to put a halt to the garbage crisis and other environmental crises, is to reduce the human population on the planet. This, of course, will be up to you and your generation.

Population scientists now estimate that the earth's population will reach 10 billion people by the year 2029. Right now, there are 5.4 billion people on earth. What will it be like with 10 billion people? Yet, if every family, starting right now, were to have only two children, the earth's population growth would level off at about 9 billion people in 25 years. This will not end the stress on the environment, but it is a start to help solve many of our environmental problems.

Reaching zero population growth, along with young people becoming more aware of our environmental problems, will go a long way toward starting us on environmental recovery. It is up to you. If young people do not clean up the environment, who will, and who will suffer the consequences more?

Now is the time to make a start. Your fate is in your hands. Only people can fix what people have broken. Put into practice the principles laid down in this book for reducing the garbage stream. Put pressure on our government leaders to create and enforce strict laws that regulate the packaging and manufacturing of products and that regulate recycling. If your government representatives do not adhere to an environmental approach in order to protect and preserve our natural resources, you should see to it that they know how you feel. Write to them and tell them you want officials who will protect and preserve the environment.

Industries should be pressured so they will manufacture products from recycled materials. Their products should also be able to be recycled. If an industry or industries fail to use recyclables, their products should be boycotted. This will be enough pressure to convince them to change their environmental policy.

Special taxes should be imposed on those industries, communities, and individuals who refuse to comply with recycling ordinances. The revenues should then be used for research and to pressure environmental offenders.

Heavy pressures should be put upon foreign governments who refuse to comply with worldwide environmental standards, such as recycling instead of cutting down the world's rain forests. These governments must be made to understand that they have no other choice but to comply with the standards set by the world community.

Finally, every individual must do his or her part to preserve and promote the environment. It must start with the individual. Each person on earth is an important key to environmental success. From the individual will emanate the power and the will to make this planet an environmental haven for all living creatures.

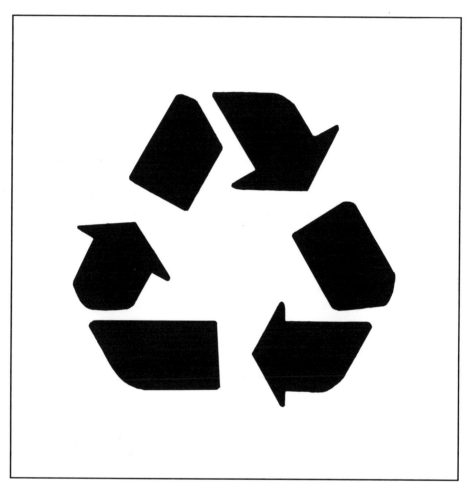

This symbol tells you that a product is able to be recycled. Many more products than ever before contain this symbol on their packaging.

It is the behavior of people that causes the environmental problems on the planet. Nature does contribute to the crisis, but very nominally. As people, with the ability to alter the environment, we have an awesome responsibility for the quality of life on earth. Today, we must decide whether to let the quality of the earth's environment deteriorate or whether to change our ways and improve and preserve the environment for years to come.

Did You Know That . . .

- In the United States, we throw away enough paper each year to build a 12-foot-high wall from Los Angeles to New York City?

- In the United States, we generate enough garbage each day to fill 63,000 garbage trucks that hold 7 to 14 tons of trash each?

- In New York City, 7.2 million people generate 36,000 tons of waste each day?

- A landfill on Staten Island, New York, currently contains 36 billion square feet of trash?

- In the Russian Federation, each person uses 25 pounds of paper and, in China, only two pounds of paper are used per person?

- It takes 17 trees to make 1 ton of paper?

- Recycling paper saves approximately 200 million trees each year?

- Residents of the state of Wisconsin throw away each year:

  > 2 billion cans,
  > 1 billion glass containers,
  > 300 million plastic bottles,
  > 500,000 tons of food waste, and
  > 4 million tires

Glossary

autotrophic—Descriptive of any organism that can manufacture its own food, specifically green plants.

bauxite—A mineral used to manufacture aluminum.

biodegradable—Wastes that are able to be broken down in the natural cycle of decomposition.

biological—Descriptive of the living aspect of the biosphere.

biome—The community of living organisms of a single ecological region; i.e., rain forests, grasslands, and deserts.

biosphere—The portion of the earth and its atmosphere that is capable of supporting life.

carbon cycle—The manner in which carbon (one element found in every living thing) is cycled, through the food chain, to all living things.

carrying capacity—The maximum ability of any specific ecosystem to support life. If the living population surpasses the carrying capacity, then the ecosystem loses its ability to support life.

classification—Putting objects into groups.

commensalism—A form of symbiosis (close relationship) involving two or more organisms. One organism benefits from the relationship, while the other is neither helped nor harmed.

composting—Using microbes to naturally decompose yard wastes and food scraps that have been mixed with other materials. It comes from the Latin meaning to put together.

conclusion—A step in the scientific method that states whether or not a hypothesis is correct and why or why not.

condensation—Water vapor turning into water droplets.

consumers—Part of the food web. Animals that do not make their own food, but eat plants or other animals for energy.

decomposers—Animals and plants that break down dead or waste material; i.e., protozoans, bacteria, fungi, molds, certain worms, and flies.

decomposition—The breakdown of organic wastes by microbes.

ecology—The study of how all living things interrelate with one another and their nonliving environment.

ecosystem—A specialized community, including all the component organisms that form an interacting system; i.e., pond, marsh, bog, or wood lot.

energy—The ability to do work.

evaporate—The process through which water goes into the air as water vapor.

finite—Has an end; cannot go on forever.

food web—The relationship of organisms within a community and their dependence upon one another for energy in the form of food.

fossil fuel—Any fuel derived from the fossil remains of plants or animals; i.e., coal, oil, and natural gas.

garbage—Soiled or waste food that is thrown away; sometimes referred to as "wet food waste" (does not include dry materials—trash).

glassphalt—A combination of crushed glass and asphalt.

groundwater—Water standing in or moving through the soil and underlying areas.

herbivore—Any animal that only eats plants.

heterotrophic—Descriptive of any organism that cannot manufacture its own food; i.e., green plants.

host—In parasitism, the organism which is harmed.

humus—Organic material consisting of decayed vegetable matter that provides nutrients for plants and increases the ability of the soil to retain water.

hydrologic cycle—The system by which water is cycled about the planet Earth: evaporation, condensation, precipitation.

hypothesis—In the scientific method, an inference or prediction that can be tested.

incineration—The process of burning solid waste; often done to recover energy.

inference—In the scientific method, an educated guess, based upon what you have observed, about something that has happened.

infinite—Without end.

interface—In ecology, where air, water, soil, and light energy are commingled in the proper proportions to support life.

landfill—A site for controlled burial of solid waste.

leachate—Liquid that has percolated through solid waste and/or been generated by solid waste decomposition and contains extracted, dissolved, or suspended materials; may contaminate groundwater or surface water.

microscopic—Any object that can only be observed under a microscope.

microbes—Any of many microscopic organisms; i.e., bacteria, fungi, protozoans, etc.

mutualism—In symbiosis, a relationship between two or more organisms where both organisms benefit.

natural resource—Valuable naturally occurring material; i.e., soil, trees, air, water, and fossil fuels.

nitrate (NO_3)—A compound of nitrogen useable by green plants; absorbed through roots from the soil.

nitrogen cycle—The way in which nitrogen is passed on to living organisms.

nonrenewable resource—Any substance available only in limited amounts. These substances may also take many years to develop and, therefore, they are nonreplaceable.

nutrients—Necessary minerals used by living things to carry on their life processes.

observing—In the scientific method, using all your senses to find out all you can.

omnivore—Any organism that eats both meat and plants; i.e., bears, raccoons, and people.

organic matter—Refers to living substances or waste from living substances.

oxygen(O)—A gas that makes up 21 percent of the air; almost all living things require oxygen to exist.

parasite—In symbiosis, the organism in parasitism that benefits from the relationship.

parasitism—In symbiosis, a relationship involving two or more organisms in which one organism benefits and the other organism is harmed.

percolate—Refers to water running into the soil.

photosynthesis—The process by which green plants make food in the form of a simple sugar, glucose ($C_6H_{12}O_6$).

physical—Relating to nature and the laws of nature.

pollution—The state of being impure or contaminated.

precycle—Reducing waste before you buy, by purchasing products that are not wasteful in their packaging or their use.

predator—Any animal that must hunt and kill its food.

prediction—In the scientific method, an educated guess, based upon what you have observed, about something that is going to happen.

property—Something that belongs to an object that helps one to identify the object.

protein—Any of a number of naturally occurring extremely complex combinations of amino acids that contain the elements carbon, hydrogen, nitrogen, oxygen, etc.; proteins are essential to all living cells.

protozoan—A one-celled animal that aids in the decomposition of organic matter.

recover energy—Any method of recapturing energy from garbage, usually through incineration.

recycle—Any method of reprocessing and using products over again.

reduce—To make something smaller; diminish.

renewable resource—Any resource that is derived from an endless or cyclical source.

respiration—The physical and chemical processes by which an organism supplies its cells and tissues with oxygen needed for metabolism (burning food) and releases carbon dioxide gas formed in energy-producing reactions.

results—In the scientific method, the logging of what happened in your experiment.

reuse—The process of using materials over again instead of putting them into the waste stream.

solid waste—All compact wastes, including: trash, garbage, yard wastes, ashes, industrial wastes, swill, demolition and construction wastes, and household discards, such as appliances, furniture, and equipment.

surface water—All water visible on the face of the earth; i.e., ponds, rivers, and streams.

symbiosis—A close relationship between two or more living things. Symbiosis takes three forms: mutualism, commensalism, and parasitism.

technology—The application of science to industry.

transpiration—The process through which water from plants goes into the air as water vapor.

trash—Materials considered worthless, unnecessary, or offensive that are usually thrown away.

virgin materials—Materials that have not been used before; nonrecycled materials.

water vapor—Water in the form of a gas.

Where to Write

Government Agencies

Department of Interior
1800 D Street NW
Washington, DC 20240

Environmental Protection
Agency
Public Information Center
401 M Street SW
Washington, DC 20235

Consumer Groups

Aluminum Association
818 Connecticut Avenue NW
Washington, DC 20006

American Nuclear Energy
Council
410 First Street SE
Washington, DC 20003

American Paper Institute
260 Madison Avenue
New York, NY 10016

American Petroleum
Institute
1220 L Street NW
Washington, DC 20005

Can Manufacturers Institute
1625 Massachusetts Ave. NW
Washington, DC 20036

Center for Plastics
Recycling Research
Rutgers, The State
University of New Jersey
Busch Campus, Bldg. 3529
Piscataway, NJ 08855

Citizens Clearinghouse for
Hazardous Waste
P.O. Box 926
Arlington, VA 22216

Council on Economic
Priorities
30 Irving Place
New York, NY 10003

Environmental Action
Foundation
724 Dupont Circle NW
Washington, DC 20036

Environmental Defense
Fund
257 Park Avenue South
New York, NY 10016

Friends of the Earth
530 Seventh Street SE
Washington, DC 20003

Greenpeace USA
1436 U Street NW
Suite 1105L
Washington, DC 20006

Keep America Beautiful, Inc.
9 West Broad Street
Stamford, CT 06902

National Recycling
Coalition
1101 30th Street NW
Washington, DC 20007

National Wildlife Federation
1400 16th Street NW
Washington, DC 20036-2266

Nature Conservancy
1800 North Kent Street
Arlington, VA 22209

Sierra Club
730 Polk Street
San Francisco, CA 94109

Student Environmental
Action Coalition
University of North Carolina
CB 5115, Room 102
YMCA Building
Chapel Hill, NC 21599

Union of Concerned
Scientists
1346 Connecticut Ave. NW
Washington, DC 20006

World Watch Institute
460 Park Avenue South
New York, NY 10016

Periodicals

BioCycle: Journal of Waste
Recycling
Box 351
18 South Seventh Street
Emmaus, PA 18049

Garbage: The Practical
Journal for the Environment
Old House Journal
Corporation
435 Ninth Street
Brooklyn, NY 11215

E Magazine
P.O. Box 6667
Syracuse, NY 13217

Mother Earth News
P.O. Box 3122
Harlan, IA 51593-2188

New Age Journal
P.O. Box 53275
Boulder, CO 80321-3275

Recycling Today
4012 Bridge Avenue
Cleveland, OH 44113-3320

Resource Recycling: North
America's Recycling Journal
P.O. Box 10540
Portland, OR 97210

Further Reading

Books and Booklets

Alcoa's Guide to Starting Aluminum Can Recycling Activity. Pittsburgh, PA.: Alcoa Recycling Company, November, 1988.

Connecticut Citizens Action Group & the Connecticut Department of Environmental Protection. *Recycling Primer: Getting Back to Basics.* Hartford, CT.: Department of Environmental Protection, 1988.

Council on Economic Priorities. *Shopping for a Better World.* New York: Council on Economic Priorities, 1989.

Crampton, Norm. *Complete Trash: The Best Way to Get Rid of Practically Everything Around the House.* New York: M. Evans and Company, 1989.

Earth Works Group. *50 Simple Things Kids Can Do to Save the Earth.* Berkeley, CA.: Earthworks Press, 1989.

Girardet, Seymour and H. *Blueprint for a Green Planet.* Englewood Cliffs, NJ: Prentice Hall, 1987.

Goldsmith, Edward and Nicholas Hildyard, eds. *The Earth Report*. Los Angeles: Price Stern Sloan, 1988.

Gutnik, Martin J. *Experiments that Explore–Recycling*. Millbrook Press, 1992.

Hallowell, Anne, et al. *Recycling Study Guide*. Madison, WI.: Bureau of Information and Education, Wisconsin Department of Natural Resources, 1988.

Here Today, Here Tomorrow: A Teacher's Guide to Solid Waste Management. Trenton, NJ.: New Jersey Department of Environmental Protection (undated).

Keep America Beautiful (Annual Review). Stamford, CT.: Keep America Beautiful, 1988.

Lamb, Marjorie. *2 Minutes a Day for a Greener Planet*. New York: Harper & Row, 1990.

MacEachern, Diane. *Save Our Planet*. New York: Dell, 1990.

Management of Radioactive Wastes. Vienna, Austria: International Atomic Energy Agency, 1981.

Military Toxic Network. *The U.S. Military's Toxic Legacy: America's Worst Environmental Enemy* (Executive Summary). Boston, MA.: National Toxic Campaign Fund, 1991.

Naar, John. *Design for a Liveable Planet*. New York: Harper & Row, 1990.

Pringle, Laurence. *Nuclear Energy: Troubled Past, Uncertain Future*. New York: Macmillan, 1989.

———. *Restoring Our Earth*. Hillside, NJ.: Enslow Publishers, 1987.

————. *Throwing Things Away: From Middens to Resource Recovery.* New York: Thomas Y. Crowell, 1986.

Recycling: Do It Today for Tomorrow. Chicago: Amoco Chemical Company, 1989.

Scrap: America's Ready Resource. Washington, DC.: Institute of Scrap Recycling Industries (undated).

Steel Recycling–A New Era. Pittsburgh, PA.: Steel Can Recycling Institute (undated).

Toward Environmental Excellence: A Progress Report. Danbury, CT.: Union Carbide Corporation, December, 1989.

Treasure in Our Trash. Washington, DC.: National Solid Wastes Management Association, 1988.

Wild, Russell, ed. *The Earth Care Annual 1991.* Emmaus, PA.: Rodale Press, 1991.

Articles

Allen, Ted. "Big Pack Attack." *Science World,* March 8, 1991, p. 2.

Booth, William, and Debra Cohn. "Sharing the Environmental Burden." *The Washington Post,* April 18, 1990, p. A1.

Brown, Paul B. "Plastics!" *INC.,* June, 1990, pp. 70-77.

Carroll, Ginny. "Getting with the Cleanup." *Newsweek,* September 25, 1989, p. 35.

Coco, Matthew. "Plastics: Concerns about a Modern Miracle." *EPA Journal,* January/February, 1988, pp. 41-42.

Cook, James. "Breaking the Garbage Blockade." *Forbes,* November 14, 1988, pp. 98-104.

———. "The Garbage Game." *Forbes,* October 21, 1989, pp. 121-130.

Donnelly, John. "Degradable Plastics: Are They a Delusion, a Solution, or a Downright Hoax?" *Garbage,* May/June, 1990, pp. 42-47.

Easterbrook, Gregg. "Cleaning Up." *Newsweek,* July 24, 1989, pp. 26-42.

Feder, Barnaby J. "Mr. Clean Takes on the Garbage Mess." The New York Times, March.

Fisher, Arthur. "Next Generation Nuclear Reactors: Dare We Build Them? *Popular Science,* April, 1990, pp. 68-77.

Forsch, Robert A., and Nicholas E. Gallopoulus. "Strategies for Manufacturing." *Scientific American,* September, 1989, pp. 144-152.

Golay, Michael W. "Longer Life for Nuclear Plants." *Technology Review,* May/June, 1990, pp. 25-30.

Grossman, Dan, and Seth Shulman. "Down in the Dumps." *Discover,* April, 1990, pp. 36-41.

Hedstrom, Elizabeth. "Earth Day." *National Parks,* March/April, 1990, pp. 18-23.

Holusha, John. "Scientists Are Proving that Natural Plastic Is Not an Oxymoron." *The New York Times,* October 21, 1990, p. F9.

Lawren, Bill "Getting into a Heap of Trouble." *National Wildlife,* August/September, 1988, pp. 19-24.

Lippman, Thomas. "Canisters of Glass Hold U.S. Hopes for Plutonium Disposal." *The Washington Post,* November 7, 1989, p. A3.

———. "Garbage: Fuel of the Future?" *The Washington Post,* November 13, 1989, p. F1.

Luoma, Jon R. "Trash Can Realities." *Audubon,* March 1990, pp. 86-103.

Maney, Kevin. "Companies Make Products Nicer to Nature." *USA Today,* August 23, 1989, pp. B1-2.

Manning, Anita. "Communities Pitch in to Cut Garbage." *USA Today,* November 1, 1989, p. 1D.

Marinelli, Janet. "Garbage at the Grocery." *Garbage,* September/October, 1989, pp. 34-39.

———. "Packaging." *Garbage,* May/June 1990, pp. 28-33.

Paul, Bill. "For Recyclers, the News Is Looking Bad." *The Wall Street Journal,* August 31, 1989, p. B2.

Poore, Jonathan. "Kitchen Design for Recycling." *Garbage,* September/October, 1989, pp. 18-24.

Porter, J. Winston. "Our Garbage Problem Won't Go Away by Itself." *Chemecology,* September, 1989, pp. 3-5.

Ralof, Janet. "The Growing Garbage Mess." *World Book Science Year Book 1990,* pp. 57-67.

Remba, Zev. "Recycle First: Countering the Rush to Burn." *Clean Water Action News,* Winter, 1989, pp. 6-7.

Robotham, Rosemarie. "Not in My Backyard." *Omni,* September, 1989, pp. 60-64, 92.

Schwartz, John, et al. "Turning Trash into Hard Cash." *Newsweek,* March 14, 1988, pp. 36-37.

Smith, Randolph B. "Ecology Claims for Plastic Bags Are Discarded." *The Wall Street Journal,* March 30, 1990, pp. B1, B3.

Stevens, William K. "When the Trash Leaves the Curb: New Methods Improve Recycling." *The New York Times,* May 2, 1989, pp, C1, C6.

Sullivan, Joseph F. "New Jersey Thinks Again About Its Hard Line on Trash." *The New York Times,* August 20, 1989, p. E24.

"The Green Revolution." *Advertising Age,* January 29, 1991, entire issue.

"Use It Up–Wear It Out–Make It Do." *The Conservationist,* January/ February, 1980, pp. 40-43.

Von Moltke, Konrad. "Challenging the International Order: The Greening of European Politics." *Harvard International Review.* Summer, 1990, pp. 22-24.

Von Stackelberg, Peter. "White Wash: The Dioxin Cover-Up." *Greenpeace,* March/April, 1989, pp. 7-11.

Wald, Matthew. "A Hitch in Plans for Nuclear Prosterity." *The New York Times,* February 12, 1989, p. E7.

———. "Running Out of Space for Nuclear Waste." *The New York Times,* October 22, 1989, p. E7.

Weisskopf, Michael. "Plastic Reaps a Grim Harvest in the Oceans of the World." *Smithsonian,* March, 1988, pp. 46-47.

Wickens, Barbara, with Deborra Schug. "The Throw-Away Society." *Maclean's,* September 5, 1988, pp. 46-47.

Witkin, Gordon. "The New Midnight Dumpers." *U.S. News & World Report,* January 9, 1989, p. 57.

Wittig, Pat. "Persistent Peril." *Organic Gardening,* February, 1989, pp. 66-72.

Index